Bellow & Hiss

New Women's Voices Series No. 173

poems by

Alyson Gold Weinberg

Finishing Line Press
Georgetown, Kentucky

Bellow & Hiss

ACKNOWLEDGMENTS

I am grateful to the following journals for publishing my poems, sometimes
in earlier versions:

Coneflower Café, "Dieffenbachia"
The Best of Choeofpleirn Press: Winter 2021, "Dieffenbachia" (2021 Derick
Burleson Poetry Prize)
december, "Back to the Body" (2021 Jeff Marks Memorial Poetry Prize,
judged by Carl Phillips)
District Fray, "Waterlilies Do Not Have Surface Leaves During Winter"
(2021 The Inner Loop Poetry Prize, judged by Jose Padua)
Movable Type, "Ars Pandemica"
Tiny Seed Literary Journal, "Le Futur Proche"
The New Guard Review Online, "Zephyr," "Don't Worry"
WWHP Writes, "Ancestry"

Publisher: Leah Huete de Maines
Editor: Christen Kincaid
Cover Art: Rachel Pruzan
Author Photo: Alyson Gold Weinberg
Cover Design: Elizabeth Maines McCleavy

Order online: www.finishinglinepress.com
also available on amazon.com

Author inquiries and mail orders:
Finishing Line Press
PO Box 1626
Georgetown, Kentucky 40324
USA

Table of Contents

For Josh, Jo, Rainie, and Pippin.
For you, I'd go around the world and back again.

ZEPHYR

A wind whipped through the church and the church was my
   childhood.
My brother wore footed pajamas. We held each other under the bed.

A wind whipped through the church and the church was a cathedral
   and cardinals
flew backward. Waves of wind gusted the trees, gushed holy water
   around

their roots, and the deacons were sharp pencils and smelled like
   cherry Jell-O.
When the wind whipped through the church, babies were put in
   heavy boxes,

so they wouldn't get carried away. The wind pounded the high school
   gym,
jeering at cheerleaders, tearing at taffeta, carrying away my date and
   captain

of the basketball team. A wind whipped through the church and the
   church
was the rabbi's son—he, too, almost, got carried away. I held onto him

under the chuppah as the wind quelled into a zephyr that ruffled our
   little
girl's hair. A wind whipped through the church and the church was
   America.

ELEGY FOR ELEVEN

Can you see her,
there in the grass?
Under a tree, the child curled
in repose, sleeping but not really
sleeping, not really a child?

Head on a pillow of stone,
body (a container for pain
) looks calm. Light brown hair
waves about her face, windblown.
But the wind does not

blow. It has been trying.
She's tired. She tried.
A birthday balloon, earth-
bound, covered in finger-
prints, air leaking out. Her breast

buds and cutting molars will amount
to nothing. The wind will keep
not blowing, the bees will keep not
buzzing, and the flowers
will bloom like she never will.

DON'T WORRY

I'm not Hamlet.
For me to be or not
is really not the question.
The answer: I am and I am not

Ophelia, gathering pain
like wildflowers tucked in the hem
of my gown, tripping into cool, green
refusal, the current and the past

pulling me down.
Can you see me? A goose
in a gaggle of gravediggers?
Paddling past Hamlet, dumb on the shore,

and Ophelia, sunk, with her rosemary
and rue, propelling the story
forward, wings flapping furiously,
forgetting I can fly?

WATERLILIES DO NOT HAVE SURFACE LEAVES
DURING WINTER

Adolescent girls root for you,
extend scarred arms

toward cloying curls,
angling for ankles.

Ungently you lay,
un-resting on the surface,

always about to drown,
a daisy for every nosegay,

half in love with death.
Madness is all we get

from you, Ophelia.
Our ragged fingernails

dog-ear your pages, hearts assailed
by crushes, rashes, braces.

We wish to disappear
into wisps of verse like you.

Instead, we grow
up, gasping for living things.

STAGES OF WOMANHOOD

I.
Daddy unscrews
training wheels. Off you
go, or fly—
or fall.

You can't tell

II.
we're seventeen, we move, sweet,

horizontal

III.
husband. You
favor your Opa,
book and music lover.
I will bring you sausages and schnapps.

(Hold me like

IV.
this.) Birth is

the opposite

V.
of penetration.
First time, I gasped.

VI.
A crone's curse:
One day sex won't
matter so much—

cont.

VII.
now there is next to
nothing between my

labia. Between my ears—
blossoms upon blossoms
upon blossoms. The clitoris
does not disappear. You can't pluck it like a flower.

FRIDAY NIGHTS

The basement floods with desire.
We descend into dark water.

A disco ball, a ping-pong
table, a girl who got

her cherry popped. Who
wants to see our sweat-soaked

tee shirts? Who wants to
hear our raw, reeling yes,

our honest-to-god, our only this?
Is it weird that what we want is

for someone to open the basement door
and shed light on our shimmering motion?

PLANET EARTH IS BLUE

My tiny astronaut,
tethered to the mothership,
floated across the ultrasound

screen. The doctor said
Everything is perfect.
Then   nothing then

*malformed organs go   get her
husband.* Houston, we need to
abort this mission.   Awake,

knees in the crash position,
spaced out on Versed,
after the evacuation,

I said   *Please, I want
to see him again.*
I have learned that some

planetary nebulae are
nurseries for emerging
suns.   But some

suns arise from super-
nova explosions, the
death-throes of short-lived

stars. I caught a glimpse
of my kid's cosmic bits and
pieces, as they whizzed

by—his hydrogen
and other ionized gasses.
Then a lid closed

on a jar, on my deep crimson flash of starlight.

THIS WILDERNESS

There are a lot of places I like but I like New Orleans better.
   —Bob Dylan

In '88 you could walk Magazine Street
for miles of nothing, hungry as Gandhi,
and eventually there would appear a
health food store, temple to greens
and cereals, twig-like fibers and solutions,
earned communion for the walk home

to the habitat you call your own between
Audubon Park and the zoo. At dusk big cats
would preen and groom and roar, drown out
the growls of your holier-than-thou empty
stomach—both sounds signaling the insistence
of an animal demanding to be fed.

Yes, I nursed at NOLA's breast, lips pressed
against the Garden District's bruise-hued
clouds, body not rounding out but distilling
down to its essential, like a willow whose
very name means lamentation.
And that man—

who dashed my same path around the park,
who jacked against a tree as I ran by,
athletic shorts down around his thighs,
ass gleaming in the dawn—he belonged.
So did the plump of ducks that once
Lined the banks of the Mississippi

and sang to me from the book
of Isaiah: *You kept me from the pit, you put
my sins behind you.* For a time, I did
wholly belong to this wilderness,
voice hoarse with bellow & hiss.
That's who I was, once.

BACK TO THE BODY

I take my leave in autumn.
The light—weak tea
Left out all day,

Cold now. Evergreens
Are, thank God, still
As they were.

Bottle green, needle sharp.
Fall is a heartbreak.
And the ground—cold, too.

ARS PANDEMICA

Stitching left to right then right to left,
engaging both hands and both spheres,
the mind grows quiet, the hands come alive

with color and softness, the repetition
of movement. It's soothing, knitting.
The pressures of the present fall away like waves,

pull back to ties that bind to Mother,
to ocean. Pull Penelope back and forth
to her loom, for three years in and out

of her room to undo daylight.
Weaving is not so easy to unravel.
Knitting is knots and needles. Tangles

of blues that somehow something become.
Penelope weaves and unweaves the shroud
for Laertes. She passes the time counting

stiches, not millions of minutes, un bids
goodbye to Odysseus with each row unbinds
her work, rebinds herself to him, to Ithaca,

to a world that was and can be again.
No one can make her let go.
Penelope can make it never be so

by rending the very garment she's sewn.
Raveling and unraveling mean the same thing.
Here I am,

dashed against the rocks of a city that burns,
in a world that still turns, but barely. I am the new
Penny, who knits and unknits to shore

cont.

up her footing. In this cold time,
I make and unmake scarves to warm
the hearts of people I love. My wrists,

my fingers burn and ache—my work
imperfect, to rough, too bright, and not soft
enough. The stitches I make I must

pull out, one by one in one long motion. I must remake what is broken.

I must sadness push and pull away
with hands deep in knots. With mind
cleared of worrying thoughts. With hands

I remember the pleasure of things.
I remember the art of losing, the art
of knitting—like poetry, on blank space,

embroidering a story—no back space, no back space
—distracting from loss, tending the presence of love,
forever ending a line by beginning the next one.

ENTER THE PICTURE

Hurl into the world—
Baroque Mother in Light

Blue Nightgown rests in bloodless,
Anesthetized twilight, present,

Removed. A portrait, a prelude.
My father in uniform, in handsome, cradles

Me in crook of arm, beaming
Us home where waiting is the night

Nurse who will rise and bottle,
My parents' formula for getting some

Shut eye. In this wink, the nurse
Holds me, her smile yearns to slide

From her face, a Dali clock. My soft
Spot melts, my baby head swerves

Away from her shoulder. A mostly
Empty handle of gin turns the earth.

CUSP

I.
Crown-first into dirt,
I am mildly concussed.
Not my sport, riding—
I'm not a ponytail-swinging
girl who perfumes the
path with green apple
shampoo, who calls
me out in the summer
camp shower room:
Hey, ice cream cone tits!

II.
In the city to see *Annie.*
Dad and I
choke down chunks of meat and bun.
I hold a cold Coke to my forehead.
Does your face hurt? It's killing me!
That's what he says, his favorite joke.
It's my birthday and my gift is Broadway and
Neil Simon's all that's left at TKTS,
not some tap-dancing

III.
orphan.
Onstage and off an
awkward father and daughter
pas-de-deux: *I Ought to Be in Pictures.* Mom
would have chosen better. But this is the summer of 1981,
and she's tied up in Danbury Hosp-   getting brain-
zap-   -ital
-ped   she's tied up in Danbury   get-
ting   she's tied   up   brain-
zap-   ped,   she's my   mom   sending
smoke   signals   from the
psych ward

HISTORY

What is your middle name?
When were you potty trained?
Who was your first love?
Why do you cry?

Who am I?
Dr. It Doesn't Matter.
Neither does nurture—or nature.
I just appear. I care. I promise,

I swear I will be there.
I sees and *mm-hmms*
spouting, north to south speeding
down the *DSM-V*, riding shotgun

with Oedipus, your mother,
and the pothole in your heart.
Have a cup of something hot.
Do you like my throw pillows?

That's my landscaper, should I answer?
Do you need an earthly body?
Do you want to drown?
Have a sip of water. We still have time.

OBJECT RELATIONS

A borrowed umbrella,
meant for a daughter, cover
for a sudden storm. I return it
too quickly, not wanting
to overstay my welcome, never wanting
to over-stay or over-do or over-hope
or over-feel. Being here
with you is always to wonder
when a coalition of hearts will be over,
when we will return
to object lesson,
to absolution, to my ration of help,
to peeling the apple,
to parsing my mental health.
We are struck—stuck—wandering among
stark rows of limbs, sap, and bark.
Dark trees with their lacy fingers
lap the white sky. I'll blow your
mind, if you blow mine.
The ripe revelations
will fall. And we'll pick them up
and shine them up, and sometimes
we will eat them all
and think we are full.

SHAKE THE TREE

Are you unripe? Are you apple
or pear? Are you perfectly
firm? Are you shiny and
symmetrical? Do you know
your trunk circumference?
How much the wind weighs?
How many leaves you've left

on the ground? Do you weather or
not the rain? When there's a storm
do you stand straight?
Do you have a solid core?
Are you shady?
Have you ever been properly
pruned?—a love equation

carved into your skin? Are you
climbable? Can you hang?
Do you quietly sing?
Do you welcome children?
Do your roots trip people up?
Have you ever been hugged?
How do you feel about your bark?

NOT FOR YOU

This poem is for me.
It's mine. The syntax, diction,
music, rhyme.
Reason,
pacing,
beauty and

pause. This is my
independent
clause.
It's
not
for

you. Line
break, *emphasis*
(words unsaid).
You
don't get it, you don't get
what's in my head.

ANCESTRY

The results came in an email.
My identity, still Ashkenazi,
at once fungible. A long-held secret

gave me sisters, strangers known,
initially, by initials—K. and D.
at the top of my Ancestry

profile. To meet was to feel
familiar, as when you hold
your daughter for the first

time after you deliver. *She's mine,*
you say. *I think I'll keep her.*
We didn't braid each other's

hair, we weren't there
for early intimacies.
We are woven, anyway,

as DNA strands wend around
young conspirators,
legs tangled on the couch,

long limbs and whispers,
one twirling a curl
around her index finger.

I don't know which gene gave wave
to Katie's hair or a scientist's brain
to Dianna, or to all of us

a dark humor.
I do know we owe it to a unit of measure.
The centimorgan, that counts our blessings in the thousands.

DIEFFENBACHIA

Dad came to brunch carrying a small plant with droplets
on it from the rain. A lovely, blue-glazed pot housed it
nicely, set off its lush, white-streaked green leaves.
He didn't offer the plant as a gift. I helped him off
with his raincoat and he switched hands, pulling his
arms through the sleeves without letting go. Dad

sat across from me on one of my favorite chairs,
keeping the plant within reach, among the collectible
cookbooks. We talked about El Nino and Hillary Clinton's
presidential chances and the scandal with her email.
My husband popped his head in to offer a wooden bowl
of walnuts. Dad cracked one with a crunch, revealing two

perfect hemispheres, a left and right brain in miniature.
In the 70s, Dad owned a nursery. I loved to go there,
pour rainbow sand into glass jars—
What kind are you? I asked the plant. *She's a dieffenbachia,*
Dad answered and carried it to the table I had laid
with silver place settings, tablecloths and napkins

of embroidered white linen that belonged
to my grandmother's mother, carefully brought over
from Ukraine. Votives nestled in ancient teacups,
smoked salmon with capers, two different kinds of
cream cheese. Cherry pastry, scrambled eggs steaming
on a plate. Cappuccinos with sugar, orange slices

on crystal dishes. *Dieffenbachia is beautiful but it can be
dangerous. Also called dumb cane or mother-in-law
plant, the poison it contains, renders any who ingests it
mute*, Dad said. During brunch,
the plant spoke only once,
when we were discussing whether I had use

for my recently acquired driver's license.
If the woman needs to go places, she has legs,
Dad insisted. The plant didn't, initially, express an opinion.
But then it did, very briefly, take my mother's likeness:
I can no longer drive. I haven't been able to for quite some time.

HOW TO MAKE A POET

You can do this the old-fashioned way,
your junk or some other guy's,
put it in a drawer and let it prove.

Does it rise? Punch it down, prove it
again. Send to study with dead men
who worship hawks and alcoholics.

Do not give your poet authentic
praise. Try, *You could be Miss America.*
Say, *If I wasn't your father.*

Linger on its waist-to-hip
ratio. Tweak its nipples, be
creepy about cheekbones.

Act a bit incestuous. Absence
is good—of the mother, better—
literal death or some other, spirit

or intellect. This also works
for fairytales. This also works for
witches. Your poet needs words.

It needs curses. It will take time, but
it will find them. DO NOT HELP
YOUR POET IN ANY WAY (

important). Walk it
over broken glass. Let it
hurt. Ignore it. Ignore it.

JOY RIDE

Dad said it was fun. The drive west in their father's 1953 Buick Roadmaster convertible, he and my uncle in the jump, wind shearing their crewcuts, a glowing cigarette up front. They wore Davy Crockett hats, scratched messages with sticks in parking lots, penciled postcards in their minds, missing the signs along Route 66 that measured the distance from Brooklyn, where their mother was stuck with her heat turned off and money dried up. In the dust of motel doorways they sat, lashing each other with licorice ropes, trying not to hear what their father did with the girls he met at gift shops and rest stops, trying hard not to know.

WHERE LIES GO

On my knees, I swallowed them.
Some round, some large and jagged.

When I was a girl I gulped them down,
My narrowest places expanding,

Ignoring the tearing in my throat,
An innocent bystander to the boa

Constrictor of my esophagus. I just
Squeezed them on through, leaving

Them perfectly intact, and down
They went, each landing in the dark,

Fertile green. Seeding my young womb,
Laying it heavy. And when they eventually

Cracked open, sprouting tangles of thorns
And weeds, I thought—this is creation,

The root of everything, the ancient
Vegetation of my pain.

HOW TO MAKE A MENORAH IN BERGEN-BELSEN

You need a minyan
of matchstick men,
from fat and gristle
to coax valuable
calories for kindle.
With fingers stiff, then
to pull threads from
frayed hems,
braid them into
makeshift wicks
and fashion,
with a stolen
spoon, a cold potato,
a kindness
to hold the candle,
to consecrate
the temple,
a guttered
miracle

I DO NOT COUNT

My binding rends. I count to ten.

Scent of tobacco, a burnt offering.
I do not count lambs. I do not count loose sheets

falling away. Who could put them back in order?
Somewhere there is daylight, and night is

here and there are scribbles in my margins.

The ceiling is a map for shadows.
I do not count stars as I float out the window.

ISRAEL IS A POEM IN CONSTANT STATE OF REVISION

We want to see the whole of The Holy City. Not just soaring glories to God, not just the postcard. The crumbling façades, home to second-class citizens, plain as the painted-eye murals staring up at us from East Jerusalem. Poetry feels redundant, useless in a place like this. Poetry, alone, is indigenous, grows wild, like figs and pomegranates. On trees. Prayer clouds float over the Western Wall and Al-Aqsa mosque. Israelis and Palestinians chant in unison, dissonance. Our tour guide says there's been an incident. We have to take the tunnels back. We follow him down into wet-walled, dimly-lit, bend-to-fit tunnels. Low threshold, sweat-soaked, closed-in, stained-green stone. To keep going, I puff on my inhaler. To keep going, our soles tread the heads of our ancestors. Everything is layered. We till our little parcel of the tel. We stand where we stand our ground. There is nowhere to go but forward in the dark. One child marches ahead of me and one behind. They both walk toward light on shifting holy ground.

LE FUTUR PROCHE

Don't ask me to live for a far-off future,
the prospect of falling in love again
or someday grandchildren.
Don't tell me to take walks every day like vitamins,
so I can be healthy enough for *them* and *then*.

I'll walk when I want to
see lichen's pale minty glow, dark leaves of oak.
The seasons are going to change, my children are going
to go. Don't ask me to live for my daughters'
daughters. No one knows who will die later or sooner.

Just for today, I am going
to walk to the gray-green falls, past turtles sunning
themselves in the shade by the faded footbridge.
Little dogs and women with strollers are going to walk past.
Two old Frenchmen are going to lean against the worn-in

railing and ask me
to take their picture. Donne-le a la jeune femme,
one is going to say, and the other is going to
hand me his camera, putting his arm around his friend.
I am going to write a poem about them.

FORSYTHIA

Beauty cracks us open
when we are ready

enough. Little shoots
pop through slate, bees

buzz. The sweet scent
of spring puddles and mud.

It is reliable, the rain,
the sweetness, the mud.

The yellow sun is reliable,
melting a corner of cloud.

I am writing on a cool afternoon
on a lounge chair near a blow-up

pool and fire pit and patio set
I panic-bought in twenty-twenty.

As if amusement amid
death could still bloom.

Once or twice friends
came to sit six feet apart.

Mostly little windows
were how we loved

the world.
My daughter is learning

Langston Hughes through
a window ... *sore ... stink ...*

cont.

sugar …
Louder, the robins sing.

THE WILLIAM VALE, BROOKLYN

—in the center of the long table, in the center of the courtyard,
we avocado toast our family. We haven't been together in more
than two years. Here on this lifeboat, in this sea of gorgeous, we
celebrate the effervescence of love: Chloe dots Kate's Mount Holy
-oke nose with Smith kisses. Watermelon kombucha tart funk fizzes.
Espresso martinis upper and buzz. Ruby and Dane keep a tight rein
on Bug, their rescue dog. He's a lunger. Jo is an auburn Justin
Bieber. A new constellation of tattoos has been discovered on Raina.
Everyone (except Reggie) is here. I grasp my beloved's hand, I rest my
head on my brother's shoulder. If this is how the world ends—

MIRIAM

She carries the water. She carries the music with her, carries other

women's children, elders, recollections. Strides between towers
of water pushed apart by God, containers for stonefish and angelfish,
swordfish and eel. So many tossed shells, remnants of those compelled
to leave home. They are fish stories now, revising with the tide.

The children of Israel have never before seen the sea.

Why now
does it open
to the middle
page?

Strangers to
their own miracle
trauma adheres
to them

like salt and sand. It will not be washed away. Not today. You
recognize this as Exodus, the great unwinding. The people will tell the
tale from shtetl to ghetto to tenement. Parting sidewalks with pickle
carts. Parting—parents, siblings, children—to work and starve or to
be gassed. They will tell it then. This way and that they will go, saying
God led us with an outstretched arm.

Miriam raises her timbrels, and they dance.

Alyson Gold Weinberg renders the "yearning curve" from trauma to transcendence in this, her debut, poetry collection, chosen as part of Finishing Line Press' New Women's Voices Series. Alyson's poems have appeared in literary magazines and anthologies including *december, One Art, Halfway Down the Stairs, The Best of Choeofpleirn Press, Movable Type,* among others. She is a 2021 Jeff Marks Memorial Prize finalist, judged by Carl Phillips; the 2021 *Inner Loop/District Fray* Poetry Prize winner; and the 2021 Derick Burleson Prize winner. She is also a 2022 *Harbor Review* Jewish Women's Poetry Prize finalist. When not writing poetry, plays, and speeches, and ghostwriting non-fiction books, Alyson binge-watches *Ru Paul's Drag Race* with her family.

www.ingramcontent.com/pod-product-compliance
Lightning Source LLC
Chambersburg PA
CBHW020223090426
42734CB00008B/1199